This little book is, first of all, dedicated
to my daughter, Michelle,
who taught me what being a mom is truly all about...
and to my husband, Michael,
who patiently walked with me as I struggled learning
how to be the kind of mom Michelle needed me to be.

But most of all, this book is dedicated to you —
the new mom!
May your heart be encouraged with love, hope, and God
hugs as you begin this new chapter of your life...
discovering and delighting in
the precious gift of your HeavenSent Baby!

HeavenSent Baby

A Bundle of Blessings for the New Mom

written and illustrated by

KARLA · DORNACHER

Published by

THOMAS NELSON

Since 1798

www.thomasnelson.com

Published in Nashville, Tennessee, by Thomas Nelson, Inc.

Scriptures used in this book are from The New King James Version (NKJV) © 1979, 1980, 1982, 1992, 2005 by Thomas Nelson, Inc. Used by permission. The New International Version of the Bible (NIV) © 1984 by the International Bible Society. Used by permission of Zondervan Bible Publishers. The Holy Bible, New Living Translation (NLT) © 1996. Used by permission of Tyndale House Publishers, Inc., Wheaton, IL. All rights reserved. The Living Bible (TLB) © 1971 by Tyndale House Publishers, Wheaton, IL. Used by permission. The New Century Version (NCV) © 1987, 1988, 1991, 2005 by Thomas Nelson, Inc. Used by permission. All rights reserved.

www.thomasnelson.com

Pages set by Left Coast Design, Portland, Oregon.

ISBN 10: 1-4041-0441-0
ISBN 13: 978-1-40410-441-9

Printed in China

Dear Friend,

If someone has given you this little book that must mean you are a new mom. Congratulations! And welcome to the world of motherhood. Nothing else will fill your heart with such joy and excitement as the heavensent blessing of a precious new baby. And nothing else will cause you to depend on God more than learning to mother this little one who has been given into your care.

Whether you're a first-time mom or experienced, whether your baby is adopted or was born from within your own womb, I pray that within every day you will discover, treasure, and celebrate the miracle of life and love that is now yours.

May the art and verses throughout this little book bring a smile to your face and encouragement to your heart!

With love, Karla

Congratulations!
You have been
chosen
to receive —
whether from
your womb
or another's —
this precious
gift of love
from God called
BABY!

sweet

You hold in your arms the most precious, perfect, priceless
gift you will ever receive...
a miracle wrapped in God's love and ribboned
in His infinite creativity!

This amazing gift comes in a tiny little package
but within it is a lifetime of promise and potential,
laughter and tears, hugs and hassles...
all waiting to unfold before your very eyes...
one moment at a time.

Your own life will also begin to unfold in a new way
as you discover the joys and struggles
of being a mom.
So delight in the process and enjoy the journey!

Thanks be to God
for His indescribable gift!

2 Corinthians 9:15 NKJV

May your heart overflow
with thankfulness and love
as you ponder this miraculous
gift from God above.

For you have been given
this sweet little treasure
to give your life new purpose
and fill it with pure pleasure.

So when the question comes —
if you're qualified to mother —
know this child is God's gift to you...
and not given to another.

Every PERFECT gift
is from GOD.

These good gifts
come down

from the CREATOR
of the sun, moon & stars.

James 1:17 NCV

Brenda struggled with not being able to have a child of her own, although she and her husband had tried for seven years. "Why not me?", she cried to God after hearing stories of women who got pregnant on the first try, of unwanted pregnancies, and of abusive parents. "Why them and not me?" she questioned.

It was at a Bible study, that Brenda was introduced to a retired adoption social worker who opened a door to a new chapter of Brenda's life. Even though the first phone call to the foster care agency brought a response of laughter at the possibility of a newborn being available through the Foster Adopt program, Brenda and Bob began the process.

Nine months after finishing the foster parent class, Brenda heard the words, "We have a little girl for you!" The voice of that social worker, who told her that getting a baby was nearly impossible, rang in her ears as she looked into the face of that precious baby, knowing that God had given them a miracle named *Grace!*

MIRACLE

JOURNAL

Every baby is a miracle in God's eyes!
As you hold your beautiful bundle of blessings in your arms today,
reflect on the miraculous gift of life you've been given.
Use this space to record some of the wonder of your baby's birth.

Baby's Name

Date of Birth

Height and Weight

Mommy's full name

Daddy's full name

Home Address

Hospital or Home Birth

Baby's brothers and sisters

Baby's first visitors

Mommy's favorite song

Daddy's favorite song

Baby's favorite lullabye

Baby's favorite food

Baby's favorite toy

Moments to Behold!

Spend some time beholding...

1. Wiggly toes and wrinkled soles
2. Twinkling eyes full of life
3. Tiny fingers embracing yours
4. Perfect lips pursed for pecking
5. Gurgles and burps
6. Sweet fragrance of new baby
7. Precious smiles... even if they are gas!

You are
fearfully
and
wonderfully
Made.

BABY

Psalm 139:14

15

When life seems
out of control,
prayer
helps us
remember
Who
is.

You've probably noticed by now, that your life is just not what it used to be. You might be sleep deprived, the laundry may be piling up, and you can no longer just get up and go whenever or wherever you want.

Compared to just a few days or weeks ago, your life may seem totally out of control. Within a matter of seconds your emotions can plummet from the highest peak of joy and amazement to the deepest recesses of fear and despair. And no wonder... your life has changed forever in the twinkling of time...

There will be good times and rough times during these first few months. There will be moments when your heart will want to burst from the fullness of joy your new baby brings you, and there will be moments when you will question and despair of your own ability to be a mother. There also will be moments when you feel so alone that you won't know how to feel at all.

Remember in those moments... you are never alone.
God is always with you and only a prayer away.

He shall give
His angels charge
over you.

Psalm 91:11

19

A day
hemmed in
prayer

seldom
unravels!

My help comes
from the LORD,
who made
heaven and earth.

Psalm 121:2

I knew you would love this precious baby… I chose this one especially for you. I'm so excited to see you grow together because I know you are going to be the best mom this child could ever hope for.

But I also know there will be days you will question this. In your weariness, you may wonder if you have what it takes to be the kind of mom you want to be. Trust me… you do. I know because I created you perfectly for each other. So when those moments come… and they will… remember that as faithful as the sun and moon are to rise in the sky, so I am faithful to you. I am always on duty, 24-7, so you can always count on me to be there for you! In the busyness of your day and at every night-time feeding… I will never leave your side.

Know in your heart that I have peace to give you in times of chaos and joy in the midst of the mundane. I have wisdom above and beyond your imagination that is yours simply for the asking… and I never break my promises. I will be your best cheerleader and blessing giver. When you feel like running away… run into my arms and I will hold you as my precious child just like you do yours.

Looking forward to our visits,
Your Ever-Present God and Father

The HEARTFELT counsel
of a FRIEND
is as sweet as perfume.

Proverbs 27:9 NLT ♥

It used to be that most new moms were never alone. They were surrounded by their mothers, aunts, and neighbors all ready and willing to offer help and give sage advice. God knew when He created us to be moms that we would need other women, old and young, to share this incredible journey with... to share the joys as well as the struggles... to encourage us and catch us when we fall.

Life is different today with families scattered here and there, but the need is the same.

The greatest disservice you can do for yourself and your baby is to be alone. If you do not have family or friends close by to love and support you, seek out a mom's group at a church in your area or look for other moms who live in your neighborhood and introduce yourself. They just may be looking for a friend too.

Moments to Pray!

Any time is a great time to pray and...

1. praise God for the miracle of your baby's life
2. ask for help when you feel overwhelmed
3. seek wisdom to be the best mom you can be
4. place your baby's future in God's hands
5. ask for God's protection over you and your family
6. ask God's forgiveness when you need to
7. thank God for the blessing of being a mom!

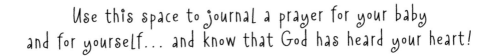

JOURNAL

Use this space to journal a prayer for your baby
and for yourself... and know that God has heard your heart!

This season of your life is like no other.
It is short and sweet and will be gone
before you know it.

Life itself is short, but the days of baby are even
shorter. In the twinkling of a moment, your baby's
gurgles and coos will turn into words, and those
tiny fingers will wrap themselves around a sippy
cup rather than the tip of your finger. And all too
soon, those precious toes you play "this little piggy"
with today will challenge you to a chase.

Today is the day to savor the moments...
to slow down and enjoy
the gift you've been given and the One who gave it.
Let all the other stuff wait its turn because
today belongs to baby.

Come to me all of you who are weary and I will give you rest.

Matthew 11:28 NLT

29

TO EVERYTHING THERE IS A SEASON

Ecclesiastes 3:1

31

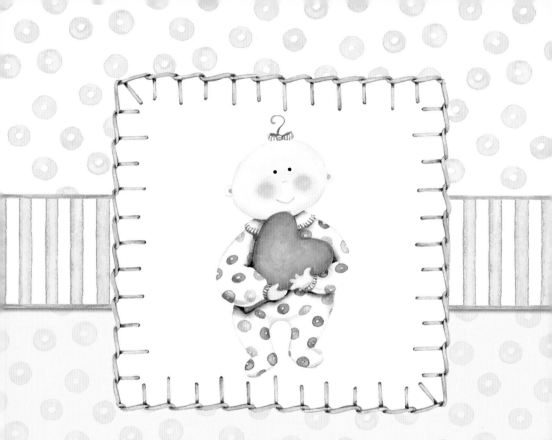

A merry heart does good like medicine.

Proverbs 17:22

Your life has changed. No doubt about it. That cute little bundle of blessings has managed to turn your life upside down overnight and fill it with dirty diapers, smelly spit up, and not enough sleep to sustain life. How *fun* is that?

Okay, fun may not be the right word... but how about *funny*? It could be. So much of life is determined by how we respond to it. If we will look for the humor in our circumstances, we can sometimes lighten the burdens of the day simply by choosing to smile instead of frown.

This is a season and it too shall pass. So let go of the to-do lists, the need for a perfectly clean house, and the drive to have it all together. You'll be able to get back to that soon enough. But for today, look for some humor in the midst of the mess, and laugh... it will make your heart feel better!

Babies Don't Stay Babies Forever!

Cleaning and scrubbing can wait till tomorrow...
for babies grow up, we've learned to our sorrow...
So quiet down, cobwebs- dust, go to sleep...
I'm rocking my baby and babies don't keep!!

35

Moments to Cherish!

Only in this season will your baby...

1. be 100% dependent on you
2. think you are the center of the universe
3. let you play "this little piggy" with his or her toes
4. drink from the breast or bottle
5. be so innocent
6. let you oooh and aaaah over him or her in public
7. let you cuddle as long as you like.

What is your favorite part about this season of your life?
Think of what you'll want to share with your baby later.

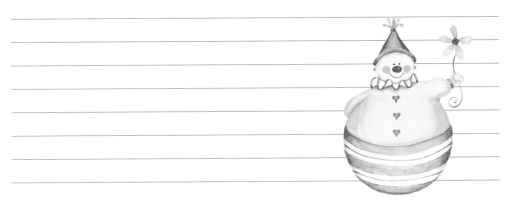

Dear Mommy,

    God created you to be a very special woman. He knew the day would come for me to be born, and in His great grace, He wanted me to have you as a mommy and you to have me as your child. I know it won't always be easy for you. There will be days you might even wonder if you have the wrong child! But even when I'm testing your patience, please know I love and need you. I am so grateful that God chose to place me in your arms, for He knew you would hold me with affection, discipline me with love, and encourage me to be the person He designed me to be. I am so happy to have you as my mommy.

        With all my heart ...
        Your baby

What's in a name? A name can shape a baby's future or forever hold a memory. Sometimes we name our children after people we love or admire, and sometimes we choose a name simply because we like the sound, which can be important since you're going to be hearing it a bazillion times in the days to come.

My daughter, Michelle, is not only named after Michael, her dad, but it's been fun to watch her grow and develop some of his nature and characteristics as well.

My older granddaughter is Alexis. While she was still in her mommy's womb, we discovered that her name meant "helper of mankind," so we began to pray and speak that character quality into her life. It has been wonderful to watch her grow and develop that very nature within her.

What does your baby's name mean? Consider praying and speaking the blessing of that name into your child's life. If there isn't a historical meaning, make up one of your own based on a character quality you'd like to see them develop and nurture it as they grow.

41

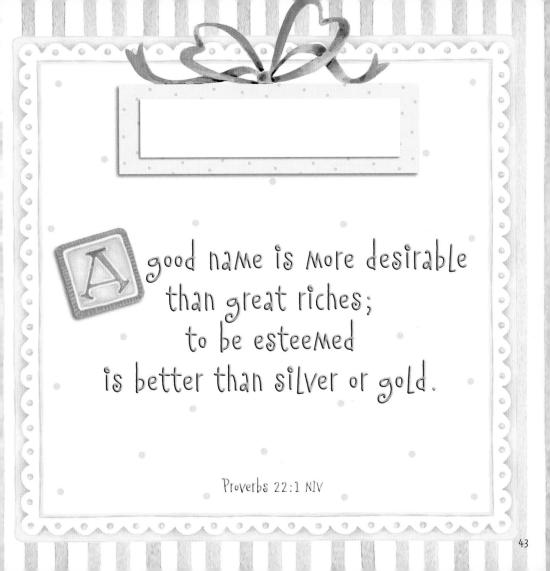

A good name is more desirable
than great riches;
to be esteemed
is better than silver or gold.

Proverbs 22:1 NIV

43

As moms, our words have the power to bless and build up as well as tear down and destroy. Your baby may not understand the vocabulary you use today, but that precious little child can hear your heart through the tone of your voice. And the words you use today to talk about your child, especially when you're tired or angry or hurt, will lay the foundation for the words you use when he or she can understand you.

Determine in your heart to speak words of love and blessing into your child regularly even now. Let your baby know that you truly do believe he or she is the greatest bundle of blessing you could have ever hoped for.

bundle of blessing

sweet

Gift from GOD

Pure Joy

Celebrate

PRECIOUS

Glorious

little one

Heaven Sent

DELIGHT

oh baby

TOO CUTE

Adorable

Beautiful Baby

special delivery

MIRACLE

45

Moments of Blessing!

Speak or pray blessing into your baby...

1. by telling them what a gift they truly are
2. by praying for the character qualities you want for them
3. by speaking the meaning of their name to them
4. by praying for them to know and love God
5. by speaking joy and laughter into their hearts
6. by praying for their future spouse
7. by speaking good things about them to all you meet.

JOURNAL

Use this space to tell your baby why you chose the name you did and what it means to you.

The heavens declare the glory of God;
the skies proclaim the work of His hands.

Psalm 19:1 NIV

By now you know that being a new mom can be...
physically exhausting, mentally challenging,
and emotionally draining.
Those middle-of-the-night feedings can take their toll
while the laundry piles up, the dust gathers,
and the list goes on and on!

Even if it means letting the dust bunnies take up
residence for this season, give yourself time to rest.
Give yourself permission to nap while baby is napping
to rest your body. Take time to pray
and give your anxious thoughts to God to rest your mind.
Place a book of short devotionals in your bathroom
to read and give rest to your heart.

It is in times of rest that your strength will be renewed
and the joy of being a new mom will be restored.

Now I lay me down to sleep,
I pray, O Lord, my mom you'll keep
and in these hours sweetly blessed
give to her a good night's rest.

As she sleeps whisper in her ear
and tell her I'm so glad I'm here!

Now I lay me down to sleep!

All babies cry. It's just normal. One study shows that the average newborn baby cries from one to three hours a day and increases crying to two to four hours a day until he or she starts to learn other ways of communicating at about six weeks. Suggestions of how to calm your baby during some of those crying times include...

1. Holding and cuddling. Your baby will learn to trust you when you respond in a loving way.

2. Walking and dancing. It's a great way to exercise while baby delights in the rhythm of your movement.

3. Music. Sing softly to your baby or try a CD of lullabies or some peaceful praise music.

4. Rocking. If you don't own a rocking chair or glider maybe you can borrow one for this short season.

5. Change position. Maybe your baby is either bored and needs a change of scenery or uncomfortable and needs to move.

Hush little baby ~ don't you cry ~
mama's gonna sing you a lullaby.

Most of us are familiar with the lullaby,
"Rock-a-bye-baby in the treetop
When the wind blows, the cradle will rock.
When the bough breaks, the cradle will fall
And down will come baby, cradle and all."

This lullaby was reportedly written by a pilgrim who watched native American
Indian moms tie their birch-bark baby cradles from the boughs of a tree
so the wind would gently rock their babies to sleep
and they would be free to prepare meals.

Not much has changed, has it? Babies need rocking and moms need a little help.
Today we place our babies in wind-up or battery operated swings
but they accomplish the very same thing.

Moments of Rest!

Sneak in a moment to...

1. Power-nap while baby's sleeping
2. Be inspired by reading a devotional daily
3. Read one chapter of a fiction romance
4. Treat yourself to a massage
5. Take a walk and delight in God's creation
6. Soak in the bathtub after baby's sound asleep
7. Phone a friend and chat about how blessed you are!

JOURNAL

What is your favorite way of resting?
How have you fit it into your busy schedule as a new mom?

In God's Time

When you look into the face of your precious baby, what do you see? And what do you dream? Have you already begun to wonder what the future holds for this wee one you hold in your arms? Can you see your child growing up to be a person who will someday and somehow change the world for good? You never know what great things may lie ahead for your child... but God does.

Whether your child was planned or a surprise, they are not here by accident. Your baby was born during this very point in history on purpose and for a purpose... for such a time as this... and so were you! As you love and nurture the character and talents of this little one... helping them know the love God has for them and for the world... you will watch their destiny unfold before your very eyes!

for such a time as this!

A PLACE FOR BABY'S FOOTPRINT

Just as no two babies have identical footprints,
no two children will be the same in nature or personality,
in talents or abilities, in strengths or weaknesses.

Our job as moms is to help our children discover the uniqueness
and the impact of the footprints they will leave.

I will send showers,
showers of blessings,
which will come
just when
they are needed.

Ezekiel 34:26

"I know the plans
I have for you,"
declares the Lord, "plans
to prosper you and not to
harm you, plans to give
you hope and a future."

Jeremiah 29:11 NIV

Jesus loves the little children
Red and yellow, black and white
Jesus loves the littl

LL the children of the world.

hey are precious in His sight,

hildren of the world.

Her children arise
and call
her blessed!

Proverbs 31:28 · NIV

JOURNAL

What are the dreams and desires for your baby?
Take a moment to journal them here.

Children are
a heritage
from
the Lord.

Psalm 127:3

Your child is a gift from God... a heritage and a reward.
This little bundle of blessings not only has the potential
to be your comfort and joy as you grow old but also to grow up
to influence, impact, and contribute to the next generation.

As you love, nurture, and teach your child in the days ahead,
imagine the virtues you want them to have, and these qualities will be
the ones you will want to model to them and teach them as they grow.

This precious child has been placed into your heart and home,
not only to have their physical needs cared and provided for,
but also for the shaping of a life.

Do not compare them to other children, but encourage them
to be the unique individual God designed them to be
and they will be more accepting of others who are not like them.
Build into your child a foundation of honesty
and they will grow to speak the truth in love.
Show them what it looks like to be caring and sharing
and they will grow up to be generous givers to those in need.
Teach them to be obedient to you
and they will grow to respect the authority of God.
Model a life of prayer and you will give them a heritage of hope
that will last a lifetime.

Savor every precious moment you can
during the first year of your baby's life
cuddling and cooing, tickling and giggling,
resting and remembering this time you have together.
For in a twinkling of a moment, this year will be gone
and the memories will become a blur.

This is a year to remember... to record... to enjoy...
but how can you do that amidst all the busyness?

Here are just a few ideas:

Don't worry about scrapbooking during this season.

But do take lots of photos, which is easy now with digital cameras and memory cards. Take as many as you like now and plan to sort them later. Be creative and try using some fun props and different angles. Don't forget to get some photos of favorite clothes, shoes, toys, etc.

Don't think you have to journal everything.

But do jot down notes that will jog your memory later and make sure to date them. Keep a journal beside your favorite chair or your bed. Maybe even keep one in your purse for when you're waiting at the doctor's office. If a journal is still too much, consider using a calendar to capture as many daily details as you have time to note.

And don't forget to write down, not only the moment,
but your feelings, so your child will know, not only who
he or she was as a baby but who mommy was as well.

Twinkle, twinkle my little Star

Heaven Sent is what you are!

71

Dear God,

I know this year is going to fly by so quickly, and as much as I want to capture the memories as a heritage for my baby, I want even more to live each moment with the greatest sense of joy and wonder possible. Give me the patience to let go of what's not important during this season so I can embrace each opportunity to sit quietly and just touch the softness of my baby's skin, to delight in that wonderful new baby smell, and to listen to the symphony of sounds my baby serenades me with.

I do want to capture as many of these once-in-a-lifetime moments as often as I can both in photos and in words, so show me where and when as a way to record the gratefulness of my heart for the heavensent gift of my baby!

With all my love,
this new mom

The memory
of the righteous
will be
a blessing.

Proverbs 10:7 NIV

74

Place Photo Here

Moments to Remember!

Special moments to savor...
1. baby's first smile
2. tickling time, bathing time, feeding time, etc.
3. baby's first tooth
4. each new skill... turning over, sitting up, etc.
5. baby's first word
6. touching baby's skin and baby touching yours
7. baby's first laugh out loud.

JOURNAL

What moment with your baby is bringing you
the greatest joy right now? Write about it here.

Other books from my heart and hand . . .

One of a Kind
by God's Design
written and illustrated by
Karla Dornacher

Down a Garden Path
To Places of Love and Joy
KARLA DORNACHER

Love in Every Room
KARLA DORNACHER

THE HEART & HOME
OF CHRISTMAS
KARLA DORNACHER

For more information about my books and gift products or to share your thoughts and comments, please write, email, or visit my website . . . I'd love to hear from you!

Karla Dornacher
P.O. Box 185
Battle Ground, WA 98604

karla@karladornacher.com

www.karladornacher.com